RAND

The Formation and Development of the Russian KGB, 1991–1994

Jeremy R. Azrael,
Alexander G. Rahr

Prepared for the
Under Secretary of Defense for Policy

National Defense
Research Institute

RAND

The Formation and Development of the Russian KGB 1991-1994

Jeremy R. Azrael,
Alexander G. Rahr

Prepared for the
Under Secretary of Defense for Policy

National Defense
Research Institute

PREFACE

This study examines the formation and development of the Russian secret police during and following the breakup of the USSR. It concludes that the Russian KGB has not been subjected to effective societal, legal, or political control and could be a significant obstacle to continued reform unless steps are taken to curtail its autonomy and power. These conclusions are based on in-depth interviews of Russian policymakers and policy analysts, as well as on published sources.

The study was conducted as part of a RAND project on the institutionalization of Russian sovereignty sponsored by the Under Secretary of Defense for Policy within the International Security and Defense Strategy Program of RAND's National Defense Research Institute, a federally funded research and development center sponsored by the Office of the Secretary of Defense and the Joint Staff.

CONTENTS

On May 5, 1991, a Russian KGB was established for the first time in Soviet history. Although the new secret police organization was initially subject to all-union, as well as Russian, command, the failed putsch of August 1991 enabled Yeltsin to transform it into a free-standing and almost completely "sovereign" institution. Hence, it was almost anticlimactic when the Russian KGB acquired full sovereignty in December 1991, with the collapse of the Soviet Union and the disappearance of the all-union KGB.

Although Yeltsin was widely expected to name a reformer to lead the post-Soviet, Russian KGB, he appointed Viktor Barannikov, a career policeman with distinctly conservative views. In addition, Yeltsin issued a series of decrees that made the Russian KGB into a near-clone of its all-union predecessor. As a result, the establishment of effective societal, legal, and political control over the KGB has been an uphill struggle.

The political bargaining power of the KGB was greatly enhanced by the increasingly bitter struggle for power between Yeltsin and his government, on the one hand, and Ruslan Khasbulatov, the chairman of the parliament, and the majority of the deputies of the Supreme Soviet and Congress of Peoples' Deputies, on the other. In fact, Yeltsin and Khasbulatov consistently tried to prevent the institutionalization of control over the KGB by "each other's" institution. At a minimum, each wanted to deprive the other of the possibility of deploying such a potentially powerful political weapon. In all probability, moreover, each hoped to be able to wield it himself. Until

October 1993, however, the KGB remained insistently *hors de combat*.

Under other circumstances, the KGB's nonpartisan behavior could have made an important contribution to Russia's further liberalization and democratization. However, Yeltsin did little to enhance the possibility of its becoming a precedent. On the contrary, he waited only three months after his political victory over Khasbulatov in the April 1993 national referendum to fire KGB chief Barannikov. Despite the hopes of the country's democrats, moreover, Yeltsin replaced Barannikov with Nikolai Golushko, a long-time KGB veteran and notorious persecutor of political dissidents, rather than with a reformer.

Golushko's first opportunity to vindicate Yeltsin's faith in him arose in October 1993, when Yeltsin disbanded the parliament and introduced presidential rule pending new parliamentary elections in December. Golushko's precise role in the "October events" is still uncertain, but it is clear that he threw his support to Yeltsin. It remains to be seen what price Golushko will try to exact for his support and whether he will succeed in exacting it. At a minimum, however, one can probably anticipate a demand that the KGB be allowed to operate with even fewer restrictions and less institutionalized accountability than it has operated with thus far.

Given how little interest Yeltsin has shown to date in the institutionalization of limitations on and controls over the KGB, his willingness to resist its demand for greater autonomy cannot be taken for granted. Unless Yeltsin throws the full weight of his authority behind the efforts of Russia's democrats to introduce and institutionalize reliable constitutional, legal, political, societal, and operational constraints on the KGB, he will jeopardize Russia's chances of staying on the course on which it has embarked under his leadership and on which he has repeatedly said it must and should continue—the course toward civility and freedom followed, in his words, by "all civilized countries."

THE FORMATION AND DEVELOPMENT OF
THE RUSSIAN KGB: 1991–1994

Many of the democrats who helped free Russia from Communist rule believed that the only way to consolidate their victory was by dismantling the huge secret police apparatus on which the Communists had relied to maintain their monopoly of power. In fact, however, the secret police has survived. Despite an official name change, moreover, most Russians still refer to the Ministry of Security as the KGB—a practice adopted in this paper as well.[1] Although the new KGB differs from its forbear in crucial respects, there are also disturbing similarities. Some of the most significant continuities and changes are examined in the following pages, which cover the period August 1991–August 1993.

BACKGROUND

Until 1991, Russia was the only Soviet republic without "its own" KGB. Like the activities of the Communist party, KGB activities on Russian territory were conducted directly by the KGB headquarters, without so much as a bow to the principle of "dual subordination" under which the KGB was supposed to operate as a "union-republic" agency. Serious discussions about the creation of a separate Russian

---

[1]The Ministry of Security was established in January 1992. Between November 1991 and January 1992, the Russian KGB was known as the Federal Security Agency. Unlike the old KGB, which combined domestic security ("counterintelligence") and foreign intelligence functions, the Ministry of Security operates exclusively on the home front. However, the old KGB's intelligence organization, the First Chief Directorate, has also survived and is now called the Foreign Intelligence Service of the Russian Federation. The activities of the latter organization are *not* treated in this report.

KGB first began in 1989, during the initial phase of the struggle for Russian "sovereignty." But it was not until Boris Yeltsin's election as chairman of the Russian parliament in June 1990 that this idea began to seem actually feasible. Immediately following his election, Yeltsin announced his intention of bringing the 70 local KGB administrations and 22,000 KGB officers in Russia under Russian jurisdiction.[2] Moreover, when the central leadership ignored his announcement, he called on KGB officers themselves to switch their allegiance to the Russian government, promising that, if they did, he would not try to employ them for partisan political purposes.[3]

It is doubtful that very many KGB officers were prepared to respond to this unprecedented appeal at a time when the center still seemed to possess a preponderance of power and authority. However, Yeltsin's threat to bring things to a head was sufficiently worrisome to the Gorbachev leadership that it agreed to open negotiations with the Russian government on the creation of a Russian KGB. After several months of acrimonious exchanges, moreover, KGB chief Vladimir Kryuchkov grudgingly signed an agreement with Yeltsin providing for the gradual transfer of all "counterintelligence" activities on Russian territory to Russian control.[4] This agreement, signed on May 5, 1991, led to the creation for the first time in Soviet history of a Russian KGB.

Although the Russian KGB initially remained subject to central command, the center's increasingly obvious inability to block the ongoing institutionalization of Russian sovereignty convinced a growing number of KGB officers that it was in their interest to obey Yeltsin's writ—this quite apart from the fact that a considerable number of KGB officers undoubtedly sympathized with Yeltsin's reformist program. In consequence, it is not surprising that many KGB officers reportedly disobeyed Kryuchkov's secret instructions to vote against Yeltsin (and for CPSU candidate Nikolai Ryzhkov) in the June

---

[2] *Radio Moscow*, December 15, 1990.

[3] *Radio Rossii*, January 25, 1991; *Argumenty i fakty*, No. 14, 1991. This call was issued in the midst of the center's attempted crackdown on centrifugal forces in the Baltic republics—a crackdown that Yeltsin had every reason to believe was the prelude to a crackdown on him and his supporters.

[4] *Radio Moscow*, May 11, 1991.

1991 Russian presidential elections.[5] More important, it seems likely that the presumed and actual "political unreliability" of numerous KGB officers was an important factor in the quick collapse of the attempted August 1991 coup—a coup in which Kryuchkov was a leading conspirator and in which other high-ranking officers of the central KGB played important parts.

The failed putsch offered a unique historical opportunity to dismantle the old KGB. Yeltsin, who was instrumental in the defeat of the putschists, moved decisively to capitalize on this opportunity, pressing for, among other things, the appointment of the reformist Vadim Bakatin as Kryuchkov's successor and actively backing Bakatin's program of radical change.[6] As a result, the months following the failed coup saw:

- The separation of the "monolithic" KGB into two independent organizations—one for foreign intelligence (the Central Intelligence Service) and one for domestic security (the Inter-Republic Security Service).

- The transfer of command over the three army divisions that had been transferred to the KGB in March 1991 and of KGB special forces such as the Alpha Group to the Ministry of Defense.

- The transformation of the 240,000-man-strong KGB Border Guards into an independent Committee for the Protection of the State Border.

- The transfer of some of the functions of the KGB's Third Chief Administration, for military counterintelligence, to the General Staff of the Soviet Armed Forces, thus weakening the secret police over the armed forces.[7]

---

[5]See *Moskovskie novosti*, No. 19, May 9, 1993, for the claim by a well-informed "insider" that 80–90 percent of the students in the KGB's Higher School voted for Yeltsin.

[6]On August 27, 1991, the reformist newspaper *Rossiiskaya gazeta* ran the following indicative headline: "The USSR KGB Must Be Liquidated." Immediately after replacing Kryuchkov, Bakatin announced that he intended to drastically curb the powers of the KGB (*Radio Moscow* in Russian, August 29, 1991).

[7]Bakatin had initially wanted to abolish the Third Chief Administration altogether but abandoned this plan because of the latter's crucial role in the protection of nuclear weapon systems against unauthorized use (V. Bakatin, *Izbavlenie ot KGB*, Moscow, 1992, pp. 90–91). Although Bakatin does not mention this in his memoirs, some functions of the Third Chief Administration clearly were transferred to the General Staff.

- The transformation of the KGB's Ninth Administration, which consisted of 25,000 bodyguards responsible for the protection of Soviet leaders, into a separate bodyguard service.

- The incorporation of the KGB's Eighth Administration, which exercised control over governmental communications and ciphers, into a new Agency for Governmental Communication and Information.

- The abolition of the KGB's administration "Z," or Fourth Department of the Administration for the Protection of the Constitution, which had replaced the former KGB Fifth Administration responsible for dealing with "political dissent."

- The dismissal of the entire KGB collegium, which, with one or two exceptions, had supported the putsch, as well as of 34 senior officials in the KGB's regional offices.[8]

- The transfer of the local KGB administrations to the sole jurisdiction of the republics.

Thanks to Bakatin's reforms (and to the drastically changed correlation of political forces that made them possible), Yeltsin was able to make rapid progress in his efforts to transform what, at the time of the attempted coup, was still an embryonic Russian KGB into a free-standing and almost completely "sovereign" organization. Whereas only 23 people had worked at the Russian KGB headquarters at the time of the attempted coup, the number had reached several thousand by late November.[9] And in the same period, the Russian KGB took over 80 percent of the central KGB's command, control, and communication systems and thereby acquired real authority over the tens of thousands of officers working in Russia's regional KGB administrations.[10] It was thus almost anticlimactic when the Russian

---

Otherwise, Yeltsin's January 1992 decree transferring them back to the KGB would be inexplicable (see below).

[8]See interview with former interim Russian KGB chief Viktor Ivanenko, *Pravda,* November 6, 1991.

[9]*Argumenty i fakty,* No. 40, 1991, and *TASS,* November 29, 1991. According to the latter source 20,000 people were working in the "central apparatus" of the Russian KGB by late November 1991.

[10]According to the head of the Moscow KGB, Yevegeny Savostyanov, there are currently 135,000 employees in "the system of the Ministry of Security, not counting border troops" (*Moskovskaya pravda,* April 23, 1993).

KGB acquired full sovereignty in December 1991, with the collapse of the Soviet Union and the disappearance of the all-union KGB.

LEADERSHIP AND ORGANIZATION

Given his strong support of Bakatin during the latter's brief tenure as head of the all-union KGB, Yeltsin was widely expected to appoint either Bakatin himself or another radical reformer to lead the post-Soviet Russian KGB. Instead he named his crony, Viktor Barannikov, a career policeman with distinctly conservative views. Of the men selected to serve as Barannikov's deputies, moreover, only one, Evgeny Savostyanov, a former associate of Andrei Sakharov, was a known reformer. All the others were veterans of the security services, including Viktor Olyenikov, a KGB officer with over 20 years of service, who was named first deputy minister; Nikolai Golushko, former head of the Ukrainian KGB, who replaced Olyenikov as first deputy minister in June 1992; Vasilii Frolov, former chief of police in Yeltsin's former hometown, Sverdlovsk; Aleksandr Strelkov, a former department chief in the GULag system; Vladimir Shlyakhtin, a former commander of border guard troops; Andrei Bykov, a specialist in scientific and technical intelligence; and two former heads of regional administrations of the KGB, Anatolii Safonov and Valerii Timofeev. Although little is publicly known about most of these men as individuals, they are clearly not the sort of people to whom one would turn if one wanted to make a clean break with the past—or even, as Savostyanov proposed, to ensure that the KGB transformed itself through a process of "repentance."[11] As best one can tell, this also holds for lower levels of the leadership, where many holdovers from the *ancien régime* were retained and many others were replaced by people of similar background.[12]

Any doubt that Yeltsin's support of Bakatin's reforms had been motivated by a desire to weaken Gorbachev's power rather than by a desire to dismantle the KGB as such was eliminated immediately after

---

[11] *Vechernaya Moskva*, April 16, 1992.

[12] Thanks to a decree by Yeltsin, most of those KGB generals who were retired were transferred to the "active reserve" and hence were allowed to keep their ties to the agency. See *Moskovskaya pravda*, September 4, 1992; *Komsomololskaya pravda*, November 14, 1992.

the collapse of the USSR, when Yeltsin issued a decree merging the secret police and the regular police into a single unified security agency that was universally recognized and widely deplored as an ominous organizational throwback to Stalinism. That Yeltsin quickly rescinded this measure when the Constitutional Court declared it unconstitutional made it clear that a return to Stalinism was not in the offing. Far from rethinking his plans for the KGB, however, Yeltsin quickly authorized a series of measures that effectively undid Bakatin's reforms and created a Russian KGB that bore a striking resemblance to its earlier all-union predecessor.

On January 24, 1992, the same day that he bowed to the ruling of the Constitutional Court, Yeltsin signed a decree returning complete responsibility for military counterintelligence to the secret police.[13] Six months later, he nullified another of Bakatin's reforms by returning the country's border guards to the KGB's jurisdiction. At the same time, he also authorized the KGB to establish its own "general staff," a step that was almost certainly associated with the KGB's resumption of command and control not only over the border guards (which had their own separate staff) but over the special troops that had been removed from its jurisdiction following the abortive August 1991 coup.[14] Scarce wonder, therefore, that no less an expert than former USSR KGB chief Kryuchkov reached the conclusion that Barannikov was in the process of rescuing the KGB from Bakatin's efforts to destroy it.[15]

OVERSIGHT AND CONTROL

Given this trajectory of developments, it was almost a foregone conclusion that the establishment of effective societal, legal, and political control over the KGB would be an uphill struggle.

Societal Control

Although some of its activities have been exposed to public scrutiny, the KGB is still far less "transparent" than its Western counterparts.

---

[13] *Radio Moscow*, January 24, 1992.

[14] *Radio Rossiya*, July 15, 1992.

[15] *Sovetskaya Rossiya*, January 28, 1993.

The recently opened and widely touted Office of Public Relations of the KGB is clearly far more interested in propaganda than in information-sharing, and most of its interactions with representatives of the independent media have been exercises in "spin control" and/or evasion. Furthermore, there appears to have been a marked decline in the willingness and/or ability of investigative reporters to pursue leads about possible, even probable, misconduct on the part of the KGB.[16] Although it is not certain how much of this decline is due to "active measures" by the KGB, it has been alleged that the KGB has offered subsidies to financially hard-pressed newspapers in return for their cooperation.[17] And the KGB is known to have threatened to arrest editors and reporters of *Moscow News* for publishing an article that allegedly revealed state secrets—"secrets" that had long since been published in the West.[18] Furthermore, the KGB's concern to prevent the disclosure of "state secrets" has reportedly led it to destroy many of the documents in the archives of the defunct USSR KGB and to fight a relentless rearguard action against the declassification of documents on the latter's oft-denounced and already well-documented crimes against the Russian people.[19]

Despite this retrograde information policy, the KGB can no longer manipulate or ignore public opinion as it once could. The momentous changes that have occurred in the balance of power between state and society have forced it to factor public opinion into its activities in a way that was completely unnecessary heretofore. The need to take account of public opinion is not the same as being account-

---

[16]There has been an even sharper decline in public protests by "insiders" against KGB misconduct. For a rare recent example of such a protest, see *Megapolis-Ekspress*, 2, March 24, 1993. In this connection, it was probably not lost on would-be protesters that two KGB officers who were imprisoned by Kryuchkov for warning that he and his colleagues were plotting a coup were kept in prison until at least a year after the collapse of the Soviet Union (see *Uralskii rabochii*, December 9, 1992).

[17]This allegation has been made by the Russian journalist Evgeniya Albats, among others. Albats made it in a talk she delivered in Washington, D.C. in late 1992.

[18]The article's authors, two scientists who described the continued production of treaty-banned chemical weapons, were arrested and imprisoned pending the outcome of a forthcoming trial. See *Stolitsa*, No. 22 (132), 1993.

[19]See *The New York Times*, July 24, 1993, p. 4, for the passage of a law adding an additional 20 years to the period during which materials from the KGB archives can be kept from the public.

able to it, however. And accountability is something Russian society has not yet managed to impose on either the old KGB or the new.[20]

Legal Control

That legal controls over the KGB have been significantly strengthened since its transformation into a Russian agency is indicated, among other things, by the KGB's unceasing pressure to repeal or amend the new laws on state security that were enacted in 1992.[21] At the same time, however, it is clear that these laws contain numerous loopholes, including some that then-interim chief of the Russian KGB Ivanenko reportedly attributed to the KGB's ability to capitalize on the unwillingness of many legislators to risk offending it.[22] To make matters worse, what was true prior to their final adoption is probably still true—namely, that where the laws are silent, the activities of the Russian KGB are still governed by the thousands of secret instructions and guidelines that governed the activities of its all-union predecessor.[23] Omissions and loopholes apart, moreover, it is

---

[20]Although the Communist party has been held at least partially accountable for its past abuses of power in various public fora, the old KGB has largely escaped responsibility despite the efforts of Russian democrats to hold enquiries into its activities and expose holdover agents and informers. These efforts did lead to the creation of a number of governmental and parliamentary commissions of enquiry, but their investigations were quickly terminated or allowed to lapse. See, for example, *Radio Rossii*, February 14, 1992, on the unrequited demand of the Democratic Russia Movement that the KGB reveal the names of parliamentarians who had formerly served as agents.

[21]The key acts in question are entitled the Law on Operational Investigations, adopted in March 1992; the Law on Security, adopted in May 1992; and the Law on Federal Organs of State Security, adopted in July 1992. Immediately after the adoption of the latter, a spokesman for the KGB called for the introduction of 18 amendments. See *ITAR-TASS*, August 27, 1992; also *Izvestiya*, March 16, 1993, and *Moskovskie novosti*, No. 18, 1993, for initiatives by the KGB for the adoption of new, much less restrictive, legislation.

[22]*Izvestiya*, January 12, 1993.

[23]Yeltsin himself ordered that until the Law on Security was passed, the Ministry of Security should continue to operate on the old directives that had been in effect since 1959. See *Rossiiskaya gazeta*, November 26, 1991, and January 30, 1992; also *Moskovskie novosti*, No. 5, 1992. This January 14, 1992, order by Yeltsin nullified a March 1991 decision by the All-Union Committee for Constitutional Control voiding all of the KGB's "secret normative statutes and departmental instructions regarding the rights and responsibilities of citizens." (*See Novaya ezhednevaya gazeta*, No. 7, May 21-27, 1993.) See *Moskovskie novosti*, No. 19, May 9, 1993, for the claim by a

far from clear that the Procuracy, which is responsible for enforcing the KGB's observance of the law, is willing or able to discharge its oversight responsibilities—responsibilities that have been expanded to include oversight of KGB operations as well as KGB interrogations of arrested suspects. Skepticism on this score is justified not only by the fact that ties between the Procuracy and the KGB have always been extremely close but also by the fact that, despite these ties, the KGB has reportedly denied the Procuracy access to its files.[24]

Legislative Oversight

If legal control of the KGB proved problematical, legislative control proved even more so. Although the Russian Supreme Soviet followed the example of the West and created a parliamentary committee to oversee the country's security services, not only the deliberations but the names of the 15 members of the so-called Committee on Defense and Security were, with only a few exceptions, kept secret. What is known is that most of its members were "experts" with extensive experience in security affairs, and that its chairman, Sergei Stepashin, himself a career policeman, combined his service as committee chairman with the chairmanship of the KGB administration in St. Petersburg until October 1992.[25] Given this situation, it is not surprising that a number of concerned legislators concluded that the Committee on Defense and Security was virtually a creature of the KGB or that one of them, Sergei Kovalev, eventually exercised his authority as chairman of the parliament's Committee on Human Rights to create a subcommittee of the latter to monitor the KGB's

---

knowledgeable "insider" that "on the whole all internal life is regulated by the old set of instructions, and many old acts have been extended."

[24]See *Nezavisimaya gazeta*, April 10, 1993, for then-Minister of Security Barannikov's claim that "the Procuracy . . . exercises strict control over us," as well as for his insistence that "transparency has limits . . . and our operational archives are not a public library."

[25]See *Sevodnya*, May 18, 1993. Stepashin was one of 13 known former or current KGB officers in the Russian parliament. See *Analiticheskii vestniki informatsionnovo agentsva Postfactum*, No. 7, May 1991. See *Krasnaya zvezda*, April 23, 1993, for an interview of Stepashin on the work of his committee. His close ties with the KGB were underscored in September 1993, when he resigned his parliamentary position and was appointed first deputy minister of security (see below).

activities.[26] Like an earlier attempt to create a somewhat similar parliamentary watchdog committee independent of the Committee on Defense and Security, this effort to subject the KGB to real parliamentary control was doomed to end in failure in the absence of stronger backing by the parliamentary leadership and the parliament itself.[27] This was all the more inevitable given Kovalev's announced determination to pursue what he considered reliable evidence of KGB spying on parliamentary critics such as himself.[28]

Presidential Control

Having elected to recreate a powerful KGB, Yeltsin might have been expected to subject it to strict presidential control, especially in the aftermath of Gorbachev's experience.[29] In fact, however, establishing such control appears to have been a difficult and inconclusive process. At the very least, this is certainly the way it appeared to two key lieutenants whom Yeltsin selected to exercise control on his behalf. Thus, both Gennadi Burbulis, who supervised the KGB for Yeltsin from November 1991 to April 1992, and Sergei Shakhrai, who served as Yeltsin's watchdog from April to June 1992, have commented that real control over the KGB is unattainable and that the latter's leadership is still in a position to impose conditions on Yeltsin

---

[26]That the Committee on Defense and Security may not be entirely a creature of the KGB is at least suggested by the fact that the only enquiry into KGB activities that it is known to have conducted identified some "failures" that reportedly required changes in administrative procedures at KGB headquarters (see *ITAR-TASS*, July 14, 1992). See *ITAR-TASS*, April 15, 1993, for the new subcommittee, which is headed by the deputy chairman of the Committee on Human Rights, Nokolai Arzhannikov.

[27]The referenced earlier attempt was spearheaded by deputies Gleb Yakunin and Lev Ponomarev and focused initially on KGB involvement in the activities of the Russian Orthodox Church. After it exposed several KGB agents and informants in the Church hierarchy, the parliamentary commission headed by Yakunin and Ponomarev was unceremoniously disbanded by the Presidium of the Supreme Soviet in February 1992 (Ostankino Television Novosti, February 3, 1992.)

[28]Interview with Radio Liberty, March 10, 1992. See also *Interfax News Bulletin*, July 30, 1993, for a similar charge by the Coordinating Council of the Democratic Russia Movement.

[29]That executive branch control of the KGB would be concentrated in the presidency rather than the premiership was never in question. According to the May 1992 Law on Security, the president "oversees and coordinates the activities of state security organs" and "makes operational decisions on security affairs" (*Rossiiskaya gazeta*, May 6, 1992).

in return for support of his reform program.[30] In effect, they confirmed that, at least on their watches, Barannikov had been willing and able to exact the *quid pro quo* that was implicit in the claim he put forward shortly after taking office: "Only the support of the army and the state security apparatus can guarantee the success of reform in Russia."[31] Although matters may have improved somewhat with the addition of a presidential Security Council to the office of the presidency in June 1992, all available evidence suggests that Yurii Skokov, who supervised the KGB in his capacity as secretary of the Council until May 1993, acted more as a go-between and mediator than an authoritative presidential overseer.[32] As for Skokov's successors, it suffices to say that Marshal Evgenii Shaposhnikov served only a few weeks before abruptly resigning and that, as of this writing, Oleg Lobov has barely had time to settle into the job.[33]

POLITICAL PARTISANSHIP

The political bargaining power of the KGB has obviously been greatly enhanced by the increasingly bitter struggle for power between Yeltsin and his government on the one hand, and Ruslan Khasbulatov, the chairman of the parliament and the majority of the deputies of the Supreme Soviet and Congress of Peoples' Deputies, on the other. It was not only that this struggle made it virtually impossible to institutionalize effective political control of the KGB, as pointed out by Aslanbek Aslakhanov, the chairman of the Supreme Soviet's Committee on Legislation, Order, and the Fight Against Crime, and many others.[34] In fact, Yeltsin and Khasbulatov consistently tried to prevent the institutionalization of control over the KGB by "each

---

[30]Alexander Rahr interviewed Shakhrai on this issue in October 1992 and Burbulis in March 1993.

[31]*Literaturnaya gazeta*, January 11, 1992; *Mayak*, January 14, 1992; *Moskovskie novosti*, No. 4, 1992.

[32]See *Rossiiskaya gazeta*, July 31, 1993.

[33]Marshal Shaposhnikov's unexpected and still unexplained resignation on August 9, 1993, may well have been connected with the change of command in the KGB in the two weeks before (see below); also see *Izvestiya*, August 12, 1993). As of October 15, 1993, Lobov's appointment had been informally announced but not officially confirmed.

[34]*Rossiiskaya gazeta*, May 27, 1993.

other's" institution in the hope of monopolizing it for himself. As early as February 1992, for example, Yeltsin responded to a parliamentary decree that vested responsibility for oversight of KGB finances, personnel, and operations in the Supreme Soviet's Committees for Defense and Security by issuing a decree of his own that made direct supervision of the KGB an *exclusive* prerogative of the president.[35] Similarly, when Yeltsin asked parliament to amend the Law on Security to remove any ambiguity about his *ex officio* status as commander-in-chief of KGB troops, parliament not only rejected his request but made the first of a series of attempts to create a parallel KGB of "its own," under direct parliamentary command as well as control.[36] When this attempt failed, moreover, Khasbulatov retaliated by calling on the country's territorial legislatures to assume direct control over the KGB administrations on their territories, even though such control was legally vested in the territorial representatives of the executive branch (the so-called heads of local administrations).[37]

In waging their zero-sum battle for command and control of the KGB, Yeltsin and Khasbulatov were both clearly mindful of the KGB's instrumental role in determining the outcome of power-political struggles in the Soviet leadership. At a minimum, each of them wanted to deprive the other of the possibility of deploying such a potentially powerful political weapon. In all probability, moreover,

---

[35]See *Izvestiya*, February 7, 1992. The July 1992 Law on Federal Organs of State Security had clearly identified the KGB as "an organ of executive power."

[36]For Yeltsin's request, see *Interfax News Bulletin*, September 24, 1992. See Russian Television, *Vesti*, December 27, 1992, for a report on a meeting, chaired by Khasbulatov's deputy, Nikolai Ryabov, at which representatives of the KGB were presented with a proposal to create separate "security services" for the executive, the legislature, and the judiciary. In a move that foreshadowed this proposal, Khasbulatov had previously appointed Fillip Bobkov, formerly deputy chairman of the all-union KGB and Colonel General Vladislav Achalov, former commander-in-chief of Soviet airborne forces, to key positions on his personal staff (reported by *RF Politika* in August 1992). During the fall of 1992, Bobkov and Achalov presided over the creation of a several-thousand-man-strong parliamentary guard service Yeltsin tried to abolish after it was deployed in an unsuccessful attempt to seize the building of the newspaper *Izvestiya*. On April 28, 1993, parliament passed a law authorizing the recreation of its own independent security service—a law that Yeltsin promptly vetoed (*ITAR-TASS*, April 1, 1993, and April 28, 1993).

[37]See Khasbulatov's speech in Novosibirsk, *Argumenty i fakty*, No. 8, 1993.

each of them hoped to be able to wield it himself. Under Barannikov, however, the KGB remained insistently *hors de combat*.[38]

The KGB first signaled its unwillingness to be drawn into partisan political warfare in October 1992, when its collegium issued a highly unusual public statement tacitly condemning both Yeltsin's tentative but widely discussed plan to introduce direct presidential rule pending (clearly unconstitutional) early selections to a new parliament and Khasbulatov's proposal to create a parliamentary KGB.[39] Barannikov reiterated the same basic message in December 1992, when he told the Congress of Peoples' Deputies that the principal duty of the KGB was to safeguard the constitution and that the KGB had no intention of becoming party to a coup of the sort that both Yeltsin and Khasbulatov accused each other of plotting.[40] Nor did Barannikov change his tune in his appearance before the Congress in the immediate aftermath of Yeltsin's soon-to-prove "inoperative" March 20, 1993, declaration of direct presidential rule. In a statement that clearly distanced him from Yeltsin but was nonetheless sharply criticized by Khasbulatov, who wanted him to denounce Yeltsin and put the weight of the KGB behind efforts to impeach him, Barannikov repeated his assurance that the KGB would under no circumstances violate the constitution.[41] Lest anyone misunderstand, moreover, he made the point even more bluntly a few days later, during a rare newspaper interview in which he declared that, so long as he remained in charge, the KGB "will not let itself be drawn into political intrigues, whoever wishes that it would and whatever the

---

[38]See, however, *Obshchaya gazeta*, No. 1, April 23, 1993, for a report of intervention by the Penza KGB in the pre-referendum campaigning in that city.

[39]*Izvestiya*, October 29, 1992. This statement stressed the need to preserve constitutional order and condemned efforts to set up "parallel [security] structures."

[40]*Radio Rossii*, December 10, 1992.

[41]Russian Television, March 21, 1993. In April 1993, when "his own" parliamentary Committee for Defense and Security, which, as indicated, was extremely close to the KGB, appealed to the latter to stay aloof from the raging power struggle, Khasbulatov angrily threatened to dissolve it (*Krasnaya zvezda*, April 23, 1993). Together with his criticism of Barannikov, Khasbulatov's anger at this appeal goes a long way to refuting the contention of some analysts that the KGB's "pro-constitutional" stance was directed primarily, if not exclusively, against Yeltsin. For a contrary view, note the remarks of Sergei Gugoryants, cited on *Radio Rossii* in Russian, July 30, 1993. Also, the remark of retired KGB general Oleg Kalugin, cited in *Yezhednevnaya gazeta*, No. 21, July 30, 1992.

circumstances. Still less will it ever again become an instrument of political violence."[42]

Barannikov's determination to keep the KGB on the sidelines during the final rounds of the struggle between Yeltsin and Khasbulatov may well have stemmed from a previously unsuspected (or newfound) conviction that the KGB should be power-politically neutral in principle. The possibility that he actually subscribed to a code or an ethos of nonpartisan professionalism cannot be discounted in light of his words and his actions. At the same time, Barannikov may have been guided by more mundane, prudential, and/or circumstantial considerations. He may have believed, for example, that the outcome of the Yeltsin-Khasbulatov confrontation was so uncertain that the KGB could end up on the losing side, with all the dire consequences that could entail.[43] Or, he may have believed that the KGB itself was so politically divided that any effort to align it on the side of one of the combatants would lead to mass insubordination in the ranks, thereby destroying the organization from within and increasing the chances of a devastating civil war.[44] Although data on the political affinities and outlooks of KGB officers are hard to come by, there is no compelling reason to suppose that they were any less politicized or polarized than they had been at the time of the abortive August 1991 coup, when a number of ranking KGB officers had refused to follow Kryuchkov's orders and some KGB units had "defected" to Yeltsin.[45]

Under other circumstances Barannikov's insistence that the KGB should not engage in partisan politics could have made an important contribution to Russia's further liberalization and democratization. The prospect of its becoming a respected precedent was nullified, however, when Yeltsin decided to capitalize on his political victory over Khasbulatov in the April 1993 national referendum by launching

---

[42]*Nezavisimaya gazeta,* April 10, 1993.

[43]In light of the ungrateful fate of many of his predecessors, Barannikov may have been equally worried about ending up on the winning side.

[44]Among others, Peter Reddaway has speculated to this effect (*The New York Times,* January 11, 1993).

[45]Ex-KGB general-turned-democrat Oleg Kalugin estimated that over two-thirds of KGB officers are opposed to "the current Russian leadership" (*Chas pik,* No. 9, March 10, 1993).

an all-out offensive against his parliamentary foes. One of the first consequences of this decision was a July 27 presidential order dismissing Barannikov from his post.[46]

Although official spokesmen claimed that Barannikov was fired for malfeasance in the death of 25 border guards and for personal corruption, their explanations were widely discounted in favor of reports that Barannikov was paying the price for his refusal to condone and support Yeltsin's attempts to override constitutional limitations on his presidential powers.[47] According to some of these reports, Yeltsin had only been waiting for an opportune moment to fire Barannikov ever since the latter had refused to endorse his March 1993 declaration of direct presidential rule. According to others, Yeltsin had at least tentatively decided to let bygones be bygones until Barannikov added insult to injury by making it clear that he would also refuse to go along with any effort by Yeltsin to capitalize on his victory in the referendum by promulgating a new "presidential" constitution and ordering new parliamentary elections—actions that would clearly have violated the existing constitution and that Yeltsin was undoubtedly considering at the time Barannikov was ousted. Whether or not either of these versions is accurate is still unclear. What is clear is that they are widely believed and that the lesson they convey (and that is likely to be remembered even if they turn out to be untrue) is that political nonpartisanship is as dangerous today as it was in the past, especially for a leader of the KGB.

However regrettable it may have been from the point of view of insulating the KGB from power politics, Barannikov's dismissal was

---

[46]*Interfax News Bulletin*, No. 3, July 27, 1993. Barannikov's dismissal was preceded by the dismissal of Yurii Skokov, who had supervised the KGB for Yeltsin in his capacity as secretary of the Security Council and had also given Yeltsin only lukewarm support in his effort to introduce presidential rule. According to reliable reports, Barannikov's dismissal was followed by the unannounced dismissal of two of the top aides that he had brought with him to the KGB from the Russian Ministry of Internal Affairs. (See *Moskovskii komsomolets*, August 12, 1993; see also *Argumenty i fakty*, No. 26, June 1993, for the reported arrest on charges of corruption of Nikolai Lisovoi, the official in charge of the financial, supply, construction, and medical divisions of the KGB.)

[47]This is the explanation that Barannikov himself offered in his first public statement following his ouster. (See *Nezavisimaya gazeta*, September 1, 1993, for Barannikov's own statements on this score.)

clearly no cause for dismay from the point of view of overcoming Russia's legacy of xenophobic paranoia. Even if one makes generous allowances for the right of an agency head to overstate the case for sparing his agency from drastic budget cuts in a period of general austerity, Barannikov had issued a number of calls for "vigilance" against the allegedly widespread penetration of Russia by hostile foreign intelligence services that were not merely hyperbolic but downright hysterical.[48] Moreover, in the spring of 1993, when his political leverage over both Yeltsin and Khasbulatov was at its highest, Barannikov had proposed the adoption of new laws on security that would not only have clearly violated the constitution but would have given the KGB virtually unlimited power to regiment and mobilize society in the course of performing its "counterintelligence" functions.[49] It is hardly surprising, therefore, that Barannikov's dismissal was enthusiastically welcomed by Russian champions of an open society.[50]

The country's liberal reformers were further heartened by a flurry of rumors that Barannikov's replacement would be either Sergei Shakhrai, an independent-minded, longtime proponent of legal and judicial reform, or Evgeny Savostyanov, who had spent the past two years as a deputy to Barannikov but had maintained his earlier reputation as a liberal by, among other things, publicly disavowing Barannikov's neo-Stalinist "vigilance" campaign.[51] Yeltsin quickly scotched those rumors by appointing (or nominating) Barannikov's erstwhile principal deputy, Nikolai Golushko, to the post.[52] By doing

---

[48]Russian Television, April 27, 1992; *Radio Moscow* in Russian, December 10, 1992.

[49]See *Izvestiya*, March 16, 1993; *Moskovskie novosti*, No. 18, 1993. See also *Chas pik*, No. 8, March 3, 1993, for a report of a joint decision of the Ministry of Security and the Ministry of Communications, giving the KGB the right to monitor all telephone and telefax communications without any restrictions.

[50]See *Interfax News Bulletin*, July 30, 1993, for a claim by the deputy head of Russia's Federal Information Center that Barannikov had been dismissed at the demand of three factions of parliamentary democrats who claimed that Barannikov had started allying with Khasbulatov against reform.

[51]See *Vechernaya Moskva*, April 16, 1992; *Sovietskaya Rossiya*, May 15, 1993; *Nezavisimaya gazeta*, May 15, 1993.

[52]Russian Television, July 28, 1993. On September 24, Golushko's former post of first deputy minister of security was filled by Sergei Stepashin, who resigned his position as chairman of the Supreme Soviet's Committee on Defense and Security immediately following Yeltsin's September 21 dissolution of parliament.

so, he undoubtedly reassured KGB officers that he had meant what he said at the meeting he had convened at KGB headquarters to announce Barannikov's ouster—namely, that the dismissal of their chief was not intended to "cast a shadow" on them.[53] At the same time, though, Yeltsin confirmed his continued unwillingness to reciprocate the confidence that Russian society placed in him and his reformist program by addressing its fears that the old KGB was making a comeback.

No one whom Yeltsin could possibly have selected to replace Barannikov epitomized the reason for these fears more than Golushko. It was bad enough that Golushko had spent his entire adult life as a KGB "counterintelligence 'officer' along Fifth (ideological) Directorate lines."[54]   To make matters worse, throughout most of his career, he had clearly enjoyed the patronage of diehard opponents of democratic reforms, including Yegor Ligachev, who was party first secretary in Tomsk during Golushko's tenure as chief of the local KGB in neighboring Kemerovo *oblast'*, and without whose support Golushko's subsequent promotions would not have been possible; Fillip Bobkov, longtime head of the Fifth Directorate, who chose Golushko as a deputy; Viktor Chebrikov, who was chairman of the all-union KGB at the time (1987) when Golushko was appointed chief of the latter's Ukrainian branch; and Vladimir Kryuchkov, who succeeded Chebrikov and kept Golushko on as "his man in Kiev" during a period when only someone in whom he had utmost confidence could have conceivably been allowed to occupy such a vital post.[55] Before finally betraying these patrons by joining forces with their arch-nemesis Boris Yeltsin, moreover, Golushko earned considerable notoriety as a persecutor of political dissent on their behalf—a notoriety that his activities after joining the Russian KGB did nothing to dispel.[56]

---

[53]*Los Angeles Times,* July 28, 1993.

[54]*Moskovskie novosti,* No. 19, May 9, 1993.

[55]See Amy Knight, "Russian Security Services Under Yeltsin," *Post-Soviet Affairs,* Vol. 9, January–March, 1993, pp. 47–48; *Moskovskie novosti,* No. 19, May 9, 1993; Jeremy R. Azrael, *The KGB in Kremlin Politics,* RAND, Santa Monica, California, 1989, pp. 35–43.

[56]See Knight, *op. cit.,* p. 48, for Golushko's "reputation for being especially rigorous in combatting political dissent in Ukraine." It should be noted, however, that Golushko took a much less strident tone than Chebrikov and other high-level KGB officials in denouncing excessive *glasnost'* and *demokratizatsiia* in the summer of 1988. (See

That Golushko defected to the Yeltsin camp prior to the breakup of the USSR seems clear from his appointment as Barannikov's deputy for political counterintelligence in January 1992—i.e., immediately following the breakup.[57] Only someone who had *already* performed valuable service on his behalf would have qualified for such a sensitive position in Yeltsin's eyes. Since Golushko remained in Kiev until November 1991, it seems likely that he had served as Yeltsin's "back channel" ("behind-the-back channel" from Gorbachev's viewpoint) to his Ukrainian counterpart, Leonid Kravchuk, in the super-secret negotiations that culminated in the dissolution of the Soviet Union and formation of the Commonwealth of Independent States.[58] Although there is no hard evidence to this effect, it is difficult to see what else Golushko could have done in Kiev that would have led Yeltsin to welcome him back to Moscow so warmly. In any event, it is clear that Golushko returned to Moscow in Yeltsin's good graces and that his performance after returning convinced Yeltsin that he was someone who could be entrusted with ever-greater responsibility, beginning with the post of first deputy minister under Barannikov and proceeding to the ministership itself.

Golushko's next opportunity to vindicate Yeltsin's faith in him arose in the fall of 1993, when Yeltsin disbanded the Congress of Peoples' Deputies and Supreme Soviet and introduced direct presidential rule pending elections to a new parliament in December. Part of Yeltsin's confidence that he could take these steps almost certainly derived from his expectation that Golushko would behave differently than

---

Azrael, *op. cit.,* p. 35. For Golushko's reputation as "one of the boys" in the upper reaches of the Russian KGB who are "even more severe than their predecessors" in the upper reaches of the USSR KGB, see the interview with the former first deputy of the Russian KGB's Institute of Security Problems, Pyotr Nikulin, in *Moskovskie novosti,* No. 19, May 9, 1993.)

[57]Golushko's formal title was Chief of the Security Inspection Directorate (see *Moskovskie novosti,* No. 19, May 9, 1993).

[58]Golushko served as temporary head of the successor organization of the Ukrainian KGB, the National Security Service of Ukraine, until November 14, 1991, when the Ukrainian parliament replaced him with Yevken Marchuk (see Tarao Kuzio, "The Security Service of Ukraine," *Jane's Intelligence Review,* March 1993, p. 116).

Barannikov would have.[59] At the very least, Yeltsin presumably expected Golushko to acquiesce in his plan and place no obstacles in the way of its realization. In addition, he undoubtedly counted on Golushko to see to it that anti-Yeltsin militants in the KGB refrained from anti-Yeltsin actions. In all probability, moreover, he expected Golushko to go further by explicitly endorsing the plan and ordering his subordinates to do everything necessary to ensure its implementation. It is hard to believe that Yeltsin did not try to elicit assurances to this effect prior to Golushko's appointment, and he is unlikely to have proceeded with the appointment had he received what he considered an unsatisfactory response.[60]

It is reasonably clear that Golushko fulfilled most, if not all, of Yeltsin's expectations during the critical interval between the introduction of direct presidential rule on September 21 and the occupation of the parliament building (or White House) on October 4. Although the statement he made on September 22 echoed Barannikov in its affirmation that the KGB would permit "no infringement of Russia's constitutional order," the operative message was that he and his subordinates would "unconditionally execute" the "special directives" they had just received from the president.[61] Despite numerous rumors to the contrary, moreover, this is apparently what, in fact, took place.[62] Otherwise, Yeltsin would almost certainly not

---

[59]Barannikov's probable behavior during the "October events" cannot be reliably inferred from his actual behavior *after* his dismissal by Yeltsin. Nevertheless, his acceptance of the post of "Minister of Security" under "President" Aleksandr Rutskoi and his participation in the defense of the White House certainly suggest that he might well have disobeyed Yeltsin's orders.

[60]Although Yeltsin may well have felt that replacing Barannikov with the highest-ranking KGB professional in the Ministry of Security was the best way to minimize the risk of insubordination in the ranks, risk-reduction was almost certainly not his only consideration.

[61]Russian Television, September 22, 1993.

[62]See *ITAR-TASS*, October 14, 1993, for Golushko's denial that some of his subordinates had joined the defenders of the White House. Another unsubstantiated rumor alleged that some KGB officers had sabotaged key links in the governmental communications system on October 3 and 4.

have awarded Golushko a medal, the Order of Personal Courage, on October 6.[63]

PROSPECTS

It remains to be seen what, if any, price Golushko will try to exact in return for his support. It is indicative, however, that the KGB has already proposed a new presidential decree, "On Measures to Secure Law and Order for the Period of the Gradual Implementation of Constitutional Reform," that would greatly expand its powers.[64] Hence, there is every reason to believe reports that the KGB (and other "power structures") are exerting heavy pressure to "tighten" presidential rule.[65]

Given how little interest in the institutionalization of limitations on and controls over the KGB Yeltsin has shown to date, his willingness to resist such pressure cannot be taken for granted. Nor, if he is tempted to look for them, will he have difficulty finding excuses, even good ones, for going along during a period that is likely to be characterized by widespread corruption, high crime rates, serious labor unrest, tense inter-regional and center-periphery relations, and growing extremism on the part of right-wing political forces. Unless Yeltsin resists this temptation, however, and throws the full weight of his authority behind the efforts of Russia's democrats to combine problem-solving in these areas with the introduction and institutionalization of reliable constitutional, legal, political, societal, and operational constraints on the KGB, he will make it much harder to reach what he himself has described as the ultimate goal of his reforms. To make a long story short, he will jeopardize Russia's chances of staying on the course on which it has embarked under his leadership and on which he has repeatedly said it must and should

---

[63] *ITAR-TASS*, October 7, 1993. The same medal was simultaneously awarded to Defense Minister Pavel Grachev and Deputy Defense Minister Konstantin Kobets, who had commanded the assault on the White House.

[64] *Ekho Moskvy*, October 13, 1993; interview with Yurii Baburin, Presidential Counsellor for Legal Affairs.

[65] Concern on this score was one of the motives behind an October 22 appeal by the leadership of the Democratic Russia movement for a purge of the leadership of the "power ministries." See *Interfax News Bulletin*, October 22, 1993.

continue—the course toward civility and freedom followed, in his words, by "all civilized countries."

Yeltsin's overall record provides strong, even compelling, evidence that he is deeply committed to this vision of Russia's future. By moving quickly and decisively to "civilize" the KGB, he could do a great deal to make such a future more attainable. Reports that this is what Yeltsin actually intends to do once a new constitution and a new parliament are in place derive at least some credibility from the fact that he has identified reform of the KGB as a top priority on his "post-October" agenda and from the fact that he has appointed Vladimir Rubanov, an outspoken protagonist of KGB reform and a former deputy of Vadim Bakatin, to be deputy secretary of the presidential Security Council.[66] However, these are at best first steps in the right direction, and there is still a very long way to go.

---

[66]See *Interfax News Bulletin,* September 8, 1993; Russian Television, October 6, 1993. For a recent statement of Rubanov's reformist views, see *Novaya Yezhednevnaya gazeta,* No. 7, May 21–27, 1993, where he argues that it is naive to believe that the KGB will reform itself and calls for strong control by outside structures, and *Yezhednevnaya gazeta,* July 23, 1993, where he sharply criticizes the KGB's proposal for a highly expansive law on state secrets.